D1717130

South America

A Buddy Book
by
Cheryl Striveildi

ABDO
Publishing Company

VISIT US AT
www.abdopub.com

Published by Buddy Books, an imprint of ABDO Publishing Company, 4940 Viking Drive, Edina, Minnesota 55435. Copyright © 2003 by Abdo Consulting Group, Inc. International copyrights reserved in all countries. No part of this book may be reproduced in any form without written permission from the publisher.

Printed in the United States.

Edited by: Christy DeVillier
Contributing Editors: Matt Ray, Michael P. Goecke
Graphic Design: M. Hosley
Image Research: Deborah Coldiron
Photographs: Corel, Corbis, DigitalVision, Eyewire, Fotosearch, Getty Images, Minden Pictures, Photodisc, PhotoEssentials

Library of Congress Cataloging-in-Publication Data

Striveildi, Cheryl, 1971-
    Continents. South America / Cheryl Striveildi.
        p. cm.
    Includes Index.
    Summary: A very brief introduction to the geography and various regions of South America.
    ISBN 1-57765-964-3
        1. South America—Description and travel—Juvenile literature. [1. South America.] I. Title: South America. II. Title.

F2208.5 .S77 2002
918—dc21

2002074662

Table of Contents

Seven Continents

Water covers most of the earth. Land covers the rest. The earth has seven main land areas, or continents. The seven continents are:

 North America   Africa

 South America   Asia

 Europe   Australia

 Antarctica

There is much to see in South America.

South America is the fourth-largest continent. It covers about 6,880,500 square miles (17,819,000 sq km).

South America is a special place. It has big cities, beautiful mountains, and tropical rain forests. Bananas, chocolate, and nuts come from South America. This land also has animals that do not live anywhere else in the world.

Where Is South America?

A hemisphere is half of the earth. South America is in the Western Hemisphere.

The southern tip of South America is Cape Horn. Cape Horn is about 600 miles (966 km) from Antarctica.

The north end of South America joins to North America. Joining the two continents is a narrow strip of land. This strip of land is called an isthmus. It is the Isthmus of Panama.

The Pacific Ocean is west of South America. The Atlantic Ocean is east of the continent. The Caribbean Sea is north.

NORTH AMERICA

Caribbean Sea

Isthmus of Panama

SOUTH AMERICA

Pacific
Ocean

Atlantic
Ocean

Cape Horn

ANTARCTICA

Countries

There are 12 countries in South America. French Guiana is a territory of France. Every country except Bolivia and Paraguay touches water.

Brazil is the biggest South American country. It has the most people, too. People in Brazil speak Portuguese. Another common language of South America is Spanish.

VENEZUELA

GUYANA

SURINAME

FRENCH GUIANA

COLOMBIA

ECUADOR

B R A Z I L

PERU

BOLIVIA

PARAGUAY

C H I L E

URUGUAY

ARGENTINA

Suriname is the smallest South American country. Suriname and other countries of northern South America are tropical. Sugarcane, cotton, and bananas grow well there.

Cotton plant

Banana tree

Grapes

It is drier in southern South America. Corn and wheat grow well in Argentina. Parts of Argentina and Chile are good for growing grapes. Some of these grapes are made into wine. South American wines are world famous.

Where Coffee And Chocolate Come From

Coffee beans

Cacao beans

Most of the world's coffee comes from South America. Brazil and Columbia are the top countries for making coffee. Brazil also grows cacao beans. Chocolate is made from cacao beans.

Mountains

The longest mountain range of South America is the Andes. This range is about 4,500 miles (7,242 km) long. The Andes Mountains lie along South America's west coast. They begin in Venezuela and end in Tierra del Fuego.

It gets cold high in the Andes Mountains. Some mountain peaks have snow all year long.

The Andes have the tallest mountain in the Western Hemisphere. It is Mount Aconcagua in Argentina. It is about 22,834 feet (6,960 m) high. Mount Aconcagua's peak is the highest point in South America.

Andes Mountains

Guanaco

Guanacos and vicuñas live in the Andes Mountains. They are related to camels. Smaller mountain animals are chinchillas and guinea pigs. One South American bear lives in the Andes Mountains. It is called the spectacled bear.

Spectacled bear

Older mountains of South America are the highlands. The Guiana Highlands are in Venezuela and northeast South America. The Brazilian Highlands are in Brazil. The highlands are not as tall as the Andes.

The Andes mountains are much taller than the highlands.

Highest Waterfall

Angel Falls is a waterfall in the Guiana Highlands. It is the world's highest waterfall. Its water falls 3,212 feet (979 m). This water comes from the Carrao River in Venezuela.

Largest Rain Forest

The world's largest rain forest is in South America. It is the Amazon Rain Forest. The Amazon Rain Forest covers about two million square miles (5,180,000 sq km). It stretches from the Guiana Highlands to the edge of the Andes. Most of this rain forest is in Brazil.

More than 2,000 kinds of butterflies live in the Amazon Rain Forest.

Rain forests get over 80 inches (2 m) of rain each year. The Amazon rain forest is very tropical. It rains there at all times of the year.

Amazon rain forest

The Amazon River flows through the Amazon rain forest. It is the second-longest river in the world. The Amazon carries more water than any other river in the world.

Amazon River

Many kinds of animals live in the Amazon rain forest. There are big, meat-eating cats called jaguars. There are vampire bats and colorful birds called parrots. Sloths and spider monkeys live in the trees. Big snakes called anacondas live on land and in the water. Piranhas and electric eels live in the rivers. Piranhas are fish with teeth.

Jaguar

Parrot

Piranha

Anaconda

Brazil nut

Orchid flowers

The Amazon rain forest may have
more kinds of plants than anywhere else.
Rubber trees, Brazil nut trees, and
orchids grow there. Some rain forest
plants are good for making medicine.

The Pampas

The pampas are grassy plains. These grasslands are east of the Andes in Argentina. They cover over 250,000 square miles (647,497 sq km). The pampas are good for raising cattle. Wild animals live on the pampas, too. There are anteaters, wolves, and armadillos.

Cattle on the pampas
of Argentina

North of the pampas is the Gran Chaco. The Gran Chaco is full of grasslands and forests.

South of the pampas are the hills of Patagonia. This land is good for raising sheep.

Sheep

Visiting South America

Many people visit Rio de Janeiro every year. This Brazilian city is famous for its Carnival celebration.

Rio de Janeiro

Carnival dancers

Carnival is a four-day celebration. It is like a big party. During Carnival, people dress up. They wear masks and flashy costumes. Music and dancing are common during Carnival. Colorful parades go down the city streets. Normal business stops during this special celebration.

People from around the world
enjoy Brazil's Carnival celebration.

South America

- South America is the fourth-largest continent.

- The Amazon rain forest is the world's biggest rain forest.

- Mount Aconcagua is the highest point in South America.

- South America's lowest point is at the Valdés Peninsula.

- The Amazon is the longest river in South America.

- The driest place in the world is the Atacama Desert in Chile.

- More than 300 million people live in South America.

- South America's biggest country is Brazil.

- Angel Falls is the highest waterfall in the world.

Important Words

continent one of the earth's seven large land areas.

hemisphere one half of the earth.

isthmus a narrow strip of land that joins two larger land areas.

peak mountaintop.

plains flat land.

tropical weather that is warm and wet.

Web Sites

Would you like to learn more about South America?
Please visit ABDO Publishing Company on the World Wide Web to find web site links about South America.
These links are routinely monitored and updated to provide the most current information available.

www.abdopub.com

Index